MYSTERIOUS PLACES

MYSTERIOUS PLACES

BY

GEORGE McNEILL

TIGER BOOKS INTERNATIONAL

LONDON

This edition published in 1993
by Tiger Books International PLC, London

Copyright ©1993 by William S. Konecky
Associates Inc.

Published by special arrangement with
William S. Konecky Associates, Inc.

ISBN: 1-85501-306-1

10   9   8   7   6   5   4   3   2   1

Frontispiece: Angkor Wat: Cambodia

Printed in Hong Kong

Contents

MYSTERIOUS PLACES

A Roman historian of the first century A.D. writing about the water supply of Rome well describes the modern's glance back at antiquity. "With so many indispensable structures for so many aqueducts, compare, if you will, the idle pyramids or the useless though famous works of the Greeks." As Rome's power spread throughout the confines of the known world, its contact with the vestiges of earlier civilizations provoked a definite ambivalence. On one hand, Rome venerated the strange and majestic works of other peoples and incorporated their gods into its pantheon. On the other, it looked down on earlier civilizations: the pyramids pale in comparison with the Roman aqueducts. For Romans the imperial city was the summit of human civilization toward which all human endeavor had tended.

We are in no position to scoff at this ethnocentricism, since we are guilty of the same shortsightedness. Modern man, secure in the conviction of his own superiority, looks back at the ancients and sees himself as the culmination of all history and evolution. A recent book boldly entitles itself *The Last Man and the End of History,* as if to say, "We're it. There's nothing much more to know."

Against such misplaced confidence is the growing awareness that in certain important respects modern man has missed the boat. The renewed respect and closer attention directed to imperilled indigenous cultures are reaping important benefits in medicine, ecology, and the discussion of human values.

Mysterious Places proposes to take the reader on a journey to some of the enduring monuments of earlier, and for the most part vanished, cultures. Many of these sites —the monoliths at Stonehenge, the Great

EASTER ISLAND

Statue with topknot.

Pyramids, the ceremonial city of Machu Picchu—raise all kinds of perplexing questions. How were these people capable of such feats of engineering and organization? Other places, such as Easter Island and the Nasca Valley in Peru with its prodigious landscape art, suggest even more bewildering problems. The Nasca lines may well have been engraved in the valley floor for ceremonial purposes, but they are products of a culture, like that of the Easter Islanders, that must have deeply felt the artist's sense of play, the delight in creativity.

One certain gain from this shift in perspective is the refutation of von Danikenesque theories that attribute anything impressive in ancient cultures to extraterrestrial intervention. This is western arrogance carried to the absurd. A more significant benefit may be an increasing sense of humility. Consideration of the unity of thought and attention underlying the vast temple complexes at Angkor Wat and Borobudur, the startling but liberating marriage of sexual and religious imagery at Konarak and Khajuraho, or the multiple architectural meanings of Chartres, where the church becomes an encyclopedia in stone, brings us closer to an intuition of the sacred that vivified and nourished the earlier cultures.

It is not necessary to dismiss all of Western history or escape in apocalyptic fantasies of post-holocaust survivors returning to lost states of authenticity. Western approaches to philosophy, music, medicine, and mathematics, to cite but a few examples, are all worthy of respect, and in their own way mysteries. But by encountering the mysterious legacies of other peoples, we broaden our perspective and perhaps regain a lost sense of balance. And if our renewed respect leads to active protection and preservation of these sites and these remaining endangered cultures, then future generations who will be the moderns when we are the ancients will have reason to thank us.

TREVETHY QUOIT:
CORNWALL, ENGLAND

STANDING STONES

Massive megaliths rest on ground that was sacred thousands of years ago. These stark, powerful witnesses to a bygone age are scattered throughout Europe, from the north of Britain to the island of Malta. Did they spring up independently or were they all manifestations of common cultic practices whose nature and origins are lost to us? Is there a relationship between these patently phallic monuments and the Mother Goddess figurines that are so widespread throughout the archaeological record? In their extreme simplicity of statement, these standing stones raise many complex questions.

One common thread links the most famous megalithic sites. They were all built according to careful astronomical calculations.

To build Stonehenge, which is older than the Egyptian pyramids, ancient people cut rock from quarries two hundred miles away, transported the 26-ton megaliths across a channel, down two rivers, and over land, and erected them with incredible skill. The sophisticated planning and craftsmanship over hundreds of years of construction demonstrates a correspondingly high level of social organization.

We may never know the full significance of Stonehenge or what rites were practiced there. Strong evidence indicates that one use was to expose the cremated remains of the dead to the renewing force of the midsummer sun. And overwhelming evidence exists that Stonehenge was a huge prehistoric observatory.

Stonehenge is so constructed that its standing stones provide accurate sightlines for the rising and setting of the sun and moon at the solstices. Stonehenge's neolithic astronomers could have also predicted eclipses and studied the movements of the twelve gods of the zodiac.

Carnac's 3,000 megaliths, arranged in eleven avenues, are among the most

SOLSTICE MONUMENT AT
SUNSET: MYSTERY HILL,
NEW HAMPSHIRE

*These monuments are
believed to be 4,000 years
old. The position of the sun*
*setting over the megaliths
during a solstice indicates
that these standing stones
were used as an ancient
observatory and site
of worship.*

ORACLE CHAMBER:
MYSTERY HILL, NEW
HAMPSHIRE

*This entrance to the "Oracle
Chamber" at Mystery Hill
was once topped with large
roof slabs, and the roof itself
contained two stone louvres
that could be opened and
closed. Words spoken into a
stone-lined tube in this
chamber could be heard
coming from the sacrificial
table, which is why the
word "Oracle" was used
to describe it.*

remarkable and mysterious monuments in
Europe. And across the countryside around
Carnac are scores of manmade mounds,
megalithic tombs called dolmens, and
standing stones. There is evidence that
Carnac was once the center of a cattle cult.

But, as at Stonehenge, the neolithic
builders of the Carnac countryside almost
certainly used their megaliths for astronomical purposes. The "Fairy Stone," at
sixty-five feet tall the biggest megalith in
Europe, was the central astronomical mark-
er. Megaliths and artificial mounds as much
as eight miles away were aligned with the
350-ton Fairy Stone to observe the rising
and setting of the moon. Some present-day
scientists believe that the megalithic
avenues are the remnants of a massive prehistoric astronomical instrument.

In Germany, five jagged, weather-beat-
en rocks rise nearly one hundred feet above
the Teutoburger Forest. This is the
Externsteine, a sacred place of mystical
associations. The startled observer wanders
up steps that lead nowhere and is struck by
a bizarre entrance or aperture, or a

AVENUE OF STANDING STONES: CARNAC, BRITTANY

The 3,000 megaliths arranged in 11 avenues at Carnac are in an area of France that contains the most ancient edifice in Europe, a tomb some 4,500 years old. The megaliths in the Carnac area, ranging in height from three feet to 23 feet, were used to predict the movements of the sun and moon and may also have been the center of an ancient cattle cult.

grotesque face carved into the rock. Limestone crags are filled with manmade grottoes, caves, and clefts enlarged over millennia by pagan cults and Christian monks. Modern scholars are unsure here, but we do know that ancient man used the Externsteine for astronomical observation. Near the top of one of the crags, reached only by rough stone steps and a precarious footbridge, is a mysterious chapel. The origins of its column-altar are unknown, but from its circular window the midsummer sunrise and the northernmost rising of the moon can be observed.

The Externsteine lies at the same latitude as Stonehenge, making the direction of the solstice similar at both locations. Studies have shown that there were once other chambers above this chapel that were used to observe the cycles of the stars and moon.

Unequivocal tributes to powerful cosmic forces, these megaliths have awed and inspired man for thousands of years. Whatever emotions they arouse in us, they remain seemingly unchanged, lonely sentinels from a long-forgotten past.

STANDING STONES: CARNAC, BRITTANY

The standing stones of Carnac are scattered over miles of the gently rolling Breton terrain. They dot the landscape in and around the small hamlets of Le Menec, Kermario, Kerlescan, and Le Petit Menec.

RING OF BRODGAR:
STENNESS, ORKNEY

The use of proportion and geometric relations in groupings of megaliths such as the Ring of Brodgar suggest that these ancient builders had a command of mathematical ideas, including the basic elements of trigonometry, the theory of right angles, and the concept of squares and square roots.

The five huge, weathered rock pillars of the Externsteine hold a place in German legend as important as that of Stonehenge in England. Since the time of Stone Age hunters, the rocks were a center of pagan rituals, and one peak was used as an observatory to study and worship the heavens. Later, Christian monks occupied the Externsteine's many niches, caves, and chambers.

JUNGFRAU VON DOLAU:
HALLE, GERMANY

This free standing
monolith has been an
object of cult veneration
since the early middle ages.
On one side an iron nail
has been hammered into
the rock, perhaps to ward
off evil spirits.

Though Stonehenge was abandoned by 1000 B.C., it has exerted a mystical attraction over the millennia. Earlier legends and studies claimed that the megalithic temple was erected by such diverse builders as the ancient Romans and Merlin the magician. Modern archeology has shown that it was built by local people of the late Stone Age.

STONEHENGE: WILTSHIRE

The neolithic farmers and grazers who built Stonehenge over hundreds of years were master stonemasons whose incredible skill enabled them to shape, raise, and fit together megaliths that weighed as much as 26 tons.

Stonehenge is believed to have been a huge neolithic observatory whose stones were aligned for such important events as the rising and setting of the sun and moon during the summer and winter solstices. The megalithic monument was also used to study the heavens and predict eclipses.

LOST CITIES

Imagine struggling through almost impenetrable mountains in the Jordanian desert, then passing through a dark narrow gorge and suddenly emerging in front of a sun-lit, dusky red temple whose existence had been totally forgotten. This happened, in 1812, to a young explorer named Johann Burckhardt. He had come upon Petra, the "rose red city, half as old as time."

The temple that confronted Burckhardt was carved out of the living rock. It is called the *Khazneh*, or Treasury, because of a legendary treasure that is supposedly hidden there. It stands on the outskirts of a ruined city that was the center of a great trading empire 2,500 years ago. At its zenith the city was home to perhaps as many as 20,000 people. In A.D. 106 it was conquered by Rome and remained part of the Empire until the great wave of Arab expansion. Then it was swallowed up by the desert and for over a thousand years was known only to wandering tribes of Bedouins.

Yale University's Hiram Bingham followed a Peruvian peasant up a rugged jungle mountainside, over swaying rope suspension bridges, and arrived at the vegetation-encrusted city of Machu Picchu. Perched on a ledge 7,000 feet high in the Andes Mountains, it is one of the world's most awe-inspiring and mysterious cities.

For Bingham, the initial discovery must have been much as Pablo Neruda describes in his great poem, "The Heights of Machu Picchu":

Then up the ladder of the earth I climbed through the barbed jungle's thicket until I reached you Machu Picchu.

Tall city of stepped stone...

High reef of the human dawn.

No one knows the origins of this place, only that the Inca people who conceived and built such a monumental complex of palaces, observatories, temples, and tombs

without either draft animals or the wheel were among the master builders of all time. Just as inexplicable is the sudden abandonment of the site in the fifteenth century.

There has never been a more obsessive search for a lost city than that of Heinrich Schliemann for Troy. Schliemann, an amateur archaeologist, infuriated the professionals with his insistence that Troy's ruins were located near the Turkish town of Hissarlik.

Schliemann excavated the site despite the chorus of derision, and in 1873 he found what he called the "Treasure of Priam" (Troy's king during the Greek siege). Schliemann's wife was photographed wearing the "Jewels of Helen": golden necklaces, earrings, bracelets, diadems, and headbands.

Although the remains of nine cities rest on one another at the site of Troy, it is Homer's city of Hector, Paris, and Aeneas that engaged the archaeologist's imagination as it has countless others. Schliemann's excavations and those of his successors have confirmed much of the historical accuracy of Homer's account.

The ruined cities and temples of the Aztec Empire are impressive archaeological sites, but the Aztecs themselves discovered the ruins of the magnificent ancient city of Teotihuacan. When the Spanish conquistadors—already amazed by Aztec building—were shown the lost city of Teotihuacan by the Aztecs, they were told that such a place could only have been built by giants.

A visitor today discovering the ruins of this Mexican city that predated Christ and once spread over eight square miles can gaze on the Pyramid of the Sun and the Pyramid of the Moon and imagine that giants might have built it. The Sun Temple's base is larger than that of Egypt's Great Pyramid. We still don't know who built Teotihuacan and what fate befell this city of 200,000 people.

There was a settlement at Knossos on the coast of Crete 5,000 years ago. At the height of their power and grandeur, the

COLUMN WITH CARVING: PERSEPOLIS, IRAN

This city of Darius the Great and his son, Xerxes, was marked by a harmony of architecture and sculpture that borrowed from the many styles of the vast empire and were fused into a Persian originality.

Minoan people had a vast sea empire. Their royal palace of some 1,500 rooms was adorned with delicate frescoes depicting their joy in life and housed a drainage and sanitary system that was not equaled until Victorian England. Then, around 1,250 B.C., Knossos suddenly vanished and its splendor was lost from sight until the late nineteenth-century excavations and reconstructions of Sir Arthur Evans.

The lost city of Knossos is steeped in myth and mystery. What is the truth about the Minotaur—half-man, half-bull—in the labyrinth of Knossos? Did a volcanic explosion on a nearby island cause Knossos to vanish so suddenly?

We will never know all the answers about these lost cities, but in looking at pictures of ruins we can share the excitement and wonder of their modern-day discoverers, and in our imagination we can wander the frescoed rooms of Knossos or observe the heavens from Machu Picchu, thousands of feet above the Peruvian jungle.

STAIRS WITH STONE
CARVING: PERSEPOLIS

Persepolis was filled with relief sculpture, painted in vivid colors that faded long ago. Particularly impressive is this sculpture that depicts delegations from the 23 nations that paid tribute to the Persian king.

MONASTERY: PETRA, JORDAN

High up a faceless mountain reached by chaotic pathways and steps, this monastery was cut out of the rock. It is over 130 feet high and 150 feet wide and was occupied by hermits at the beginning of the Christian era.

NABATAEAN TOMBS: PETRA

The mysterious Nabataeans, originally a tribe of shepherds, settled in Petra eight centuries before Christ. The many tombs they carved into the mountains are indicative of a religion centered on a cult of the dead.

THE TREASURY: PETRA

This rose-hued monument, called the Treasury, gleaming in the sun is the sight that stuns visitors as they emerge from the dark gorge that leads to Petra. It was built during Petra's Golden Age, from 50 B.C. to A.D. 70. (And it is featured in the climactic scene of the film Indiana Jones and the Last Crusade.*)*

Persepolis was founded in 520 B.C.in what is now Iran and was destroyed by Alexander the Great in 330 B.C. Its architectural triumph, the Apadana—the royal audience chamber—featured 36 columns, each 65 feet high, some of which still loom over the barren landscape. The city was nothing more than a heap of rubble until the last century.

MASADA, ISRAEL

King Herod built a palace-fortress on this imposing peak near the Dead Sea. A small city of palaces, pools, baths, and courtyards, lavishly decorated with frescoes, Masada was seized by 960 Jewish Zealots, who held out against the Roman legions for five years. Rather than surrender, they burned the buildings and committed suicide.

KNOSSOS, CRETE

The ruins of the labyrinthine Minoan palace of 1,500 rooms at Knossos are all that remain of the ancient sea empire. The Minoans created a harmonious way of life that fused the practical and the artistic with an impressive sophistication that stretched over many centuries, then suddenly and mysteriously disappeared around 1250 B.C.

The Minoans decorated extensively with frescoes. These life-size figures depict priests and priestesses holding flasks of ritual drinks.

AMPHORA: KNOSSOS,

In the cellars of Knossos were discovered many tall stone jars that held ceremonial liquids, and each jar was marked with a different miniature seal. (Some 4,000 seals were found, indicating a highly organized system of heraldry.)

The ruins of Troy, one of history's most fabled cities, were finally discovered in the nineteenth Century by a wealthy amateur archaeologist, *Heinrich Schliemann. The ruins lie on the mound of Hissarlik, near Turkey's northwestern coast.*

AMPHITHEATER: TROY

In addition to the Troy of Paris and Helen, of Achilles and Ulysses and the Trojan Horse portrayed in Homer's "Illiad," eight other cities were built on the site of the Hissarlik mound. The best-preserved ruin is from the ninth and last Troy. This amphitheater was the result of a rebuilding program initiated by Julius Caesar.

CIUDAD PERDILLO: SIERRA
NEVADA DE SANTA MARTA,
COLOMBIA

The Tairona period of cul-
tural flowering dates from
around the seventh century
A.D. The Tairona people
dwelt for most of the year on
the temperate slopes of the
northern and western
Sierra Nevada mountains,
but they also built ceremo-
nial centers high in the
mountains. The most
famous, known as El
Ciudad Perdillo (the Lost
City) was presided over by
nahomas, *religious leaders*
who could only exercise
their functions after years
of arduous preparation.

CIUDAD PERDILLO: SIERRA
NEVADA DE SANTA MARTA

Cut into the jungle and
winding up the side of a
mountain is a stairway
that goes for many miles
and leads to the ceremonial
center of Ciudad Perdillo.

Machu Picchu: Peru

Haunting in its mountain setting, this Inca ceremonial city is a masterpiece of urban planning, stonemasonry, and engineering. The ruling class and priests practiced religious rites and studied the heavens here. No one knows why the Incas suddenly abandoned Machu Picchu.

Sun Dial: Machu Picchu

Every winter solstice, the Inca sun god was symbolically tethered to this sacred rock, called the Intihuatana, to make certain that he returned the following summer. It also served as a sun dial, enabling the priests to chart the heavens.

Tower and Princess' Palace: Machu Picchu

The tower and the Princess' Palace show Incan stonemasonry at its most impressive.

AGRICULTURAL TERRACES: MACHU PICCHU

These agricultural terraces show the precipitous drops down the craggy heights to the Urubamba River thousands of feet below. Its commanding vantage of the river valley with its defile leading to the Incan capital of Cuzco had clear strategic value.

PRIESTS' HOUSE: MACHU PICCHU

The priests dominated life in Machu Picchu and held great secular as well as religious authority.

PUEBLO BONITO: CHACO
CANYON, NEW MEXICO

*Chaco Canyon in New
Mexico was the site of a
sophisticated Anasazi society
that built stone villages—
pueblos—at a time when the
common people of medieval
Europe lived in wood houses. The Anasazi thrived until
the middle of the twelfth century, when they abruptly
abandoned their pueblos.*

CLIFF PALACE: MESA
VERDE, COLORADO

*Cliff Palace, built into a
large recess in a canyon
wall, was an important
Anasazi political, ceremonial, and trading center in
Mesa Verde, Colorado. At
its peak, Cliff Palace consist-
ed of 23 kivas and more
than 200 rooms.*

PUEBLO BONITO:
CHACO CANYON

*The most impressive of the
Chaco Canyon villages was
Pueblo Bonito, a complex of
800 rooms in four storeys.
The superb stonework and
the geometrical precision
indicate an advanced level
of central planning. Several
kivas are visible.*

KIVA: CORONADO STATE PARK, NEW MEXICO

Only men descended the ladder into the kiva, to conduct ceremonies that remain a mystery. The kivas were also places where potters and weavers worked, perhaps functioning as a kind of men's club, an escape from the largely matriarchal society.

KIVA: CORONADO STATE PARK

Wall paintings decorate this kiva, or underground ceremonial chamber. Pueblo Bonito had 37 kivas, which featured a small hole in the ground behind the hearth. The Anasazi believed that their ancestors ascended from this hole to influence their daily lives.

CENTRAL TOWER: GREAT ZIMBABWE, ZIMBABWE

This conical tower, 30 feet high, is entirely solid, has no known purpose, and is the most enigmatic ruin of this African empire. It was built of brick-shaped granite stones without mortar and shows the skill of these ancient craftsmen.

RUINED WALL: GREAT ZIMBABWE

Great Zimbabwe, 250 miles inland from the Indian Ocean, was the center of a trading and mining nation that flourished until the fifteenth century, when it mysteriously disappeared from history. It had been cited as the home of the Queen of Sheba and the remains of King Solomon's mines, though no evidence exists to verify these legends.

SIGNS ON THE LAND

The earth has been one of man's most vivid canvases, on which he has scratched and carved an impressive array of animals, figures and symbols. This worldwide panorama of graphic images and mounds on the earth's surface and in its caves includes the most ancient and some of the most enigmatic of the world's wonders.

These original landscape artists have bequeathed to us a rich legacy. Clearly, these ancient people were far more sophisticated and artistic than we imagined.

Beginning so far back in the haze of prehistory that the mind resists the concept, people dismissed as primitive not only lived in societies more complex than we have previously recognized, but they created art that is as beautiful as it is haunting. The earliest known graphic representations are at least 15,000 years old. Large and amazingly realistic representations of horses, bison, mammoths, deer, and elephants adorn the walls and ceilings of the caves of Lascaux in France and Altamira in Spain. Many are perfectly proportioned. One shows a hunting scene, another an animal in its death agony. They demonstrate such ability, sophistication, and technique that some experts insist that they could have come only after long experimentation, though no such earlier work has been found.

No one knows why Stone Age man created such art; we can only imagine magical rites deep in the caves, perhaps connected with the hunt, as people came in from their dwellings—the caves were not occupied as homes—to stare in awe at the brown, red, and ocher animals and perhaps to revere the artists of their ice-bound world thousands of years ago.

Twelve thousand years ago, the Nasca area of Peru was already settled by a people who would eventually leave in the yellow soil of one of earth's most arid places a combination of art and enigma rarely equaled in history. The Nasca people had already vanished and become legend when the Inca Empire arose, but between 500 B.C. and A.D. 500 their development as artists culminated in a massive, mysterious array of dead-straight lines, geometric symbols, and gigantic animal figures on the landscape.

These are among the most bewildering networks of land signs, indeed of any monuments, that exist from early man. Working entirely by hand—they had no draft animals—these Nasca people scraped away tons of rocks and topsoil to create such works of art and wonder as a rare Amazonian spider some 150 feet long (and so detailed that it includes a reproductive organ normally visible only under a microscope) and a mammoth hummingbird with outspread wings that is delineated by a single line. Other works scratched on the desert floor include a snake, a whale, a lizard, and a monkey.

The lines are maddeningly straight, hundreds of feet long and created for no known purpose, since some of them end abruptly on top of a hill and others lead simply nowhere at all. One of the most intriguing aspects of the Nasca land signs is that their forms are legible only when seen from the air.

No place on earth has aroused more speculation than Nasca. Some view this graphic earthen scratch pad as a massive celestial notebook and astronomical system; others offer explanations ranging from kinship pathways between sites that were revered in ancestor worship, to ancient highways; from ritual dance grounds to UFO landing fields.

In England, ancient peoples scratched away the green turf and created giant white chalk figures of men and animals. The chalk giant at Cerne Abbas is 180 feet tall, and naked, with a 30-foot erect phallus. He is a daunting sight, there in the white chalk, a blatantly erotic symbol from a time when man did not consider naked figures obscene.

His Iron Age origin is a mystery. But the fact that the giant was maintained over so many centuries indicates his importance to the local people in at least one aspect—as a fertility symbol. It was common for barren

women to sit on the phallus in hope of becoming pregnant.

The highly stylized White Horse of Uffington stretches some 350 feet from head to tail. It is a powerful image in the earth and wreathed in legend. Many believe it is not a horse, but a dragon, and Dragon Hill, where St. George is said to have killed the dragon, lies below the chalk image. So venerated was this Celtic creation that at one time it was ritually scoured every seven years.

American Indian cultures left their signs and symbols, not only painted on cave walls or carved into the earth, but in fantastic effigy mounds. Scattered throughout the Mississippi and Ohio river valleys are thousands of Indian mounds. The most impressive are shaped like birds, foxes, bears, snakes, and buffaloes. The most elaborate effigy mound, more than a quarter-mile long and some 2,000 years old, is the Great Serpent Mound in Ohio. This twisting serpent follows the bend of a stream and appears to have an egg in its mouth.

Generations of archaeologists have been perplexed about the origin and meaning of the Great Serpent Mound, since it was not used for burial purposes; but there is no doubt about the vigor, richness, and creativity of the Adana culture that created it.

Our ancestors' natural instinct to change their landscape for creative, ritualistic, and sometimes practical purposes has bequeathed us a dazzling legacy of landscape art and an appreciation for both the sophistication and the artistic endeavor of people whose cultures stretch back into the reaches of prehistory.

GREAT SERPENT MOUND: OHIO

This Great Serpent Mound in Ohio is one of thousands of mounds built by the Adana Indians in the first millennium B.C. This mound of a snake, one of several effigy mounds, was not built for the usual burial purposes and may have symbolized the common belief that the snake represented the power of water to regenerate the land.

CHALK GIANT:
CERNE ABBAS,
DORSET, ENGLAND

Celebrated as a fertility symbol for some 2,000 years, the giant at Cerne Abbas resembles a picture of Hercules found on a Roman artifact in Norfolk. There was a Hercules cult in England during the Roman rule there. Unmarried women, wishing for a marriage that produced many children, would spend the night on the giant's outline scratched into the chalk hillside.

Overleaf
WHITE HORSE
OF UFFINGTON:
OXFORDSHIRE, ENGLAND

The highly stylized White Horse of Uffington was probably created in the first century B.C. by Iron Age Celts, who worshiped the horse as a goddess. Local legend holds that the huge chalk figure is actually a dragon; if so, it may celebrate St. George's victory.

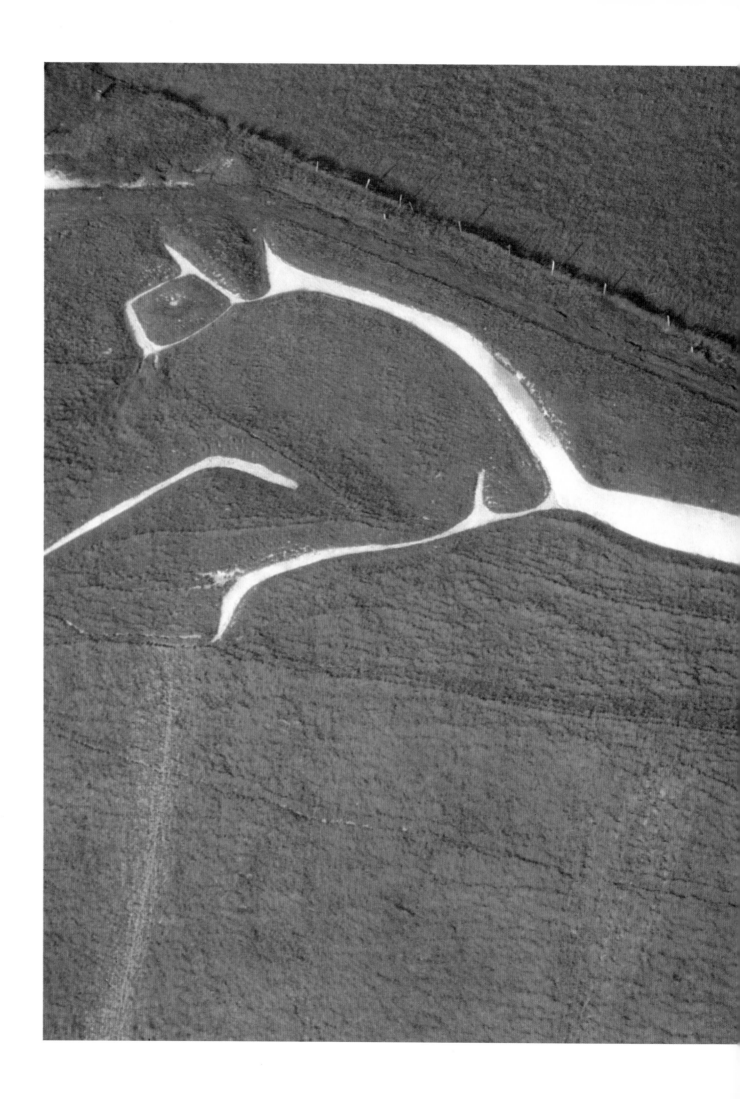

CAVE PAINTING:
LASCAUX, FRANCE

Originally, when game was plentiful, the cave paintings, often marked by lines representing spears, were meant to give men the power to destroy the animals they hunted. As game became scarce, it is possible that the paintings were used in rites intended to increase the supply of game.

CAVE PAINTING: LASCAUX

This black bull was painted between 15,000 and 10,000 B.C. in a cave at Lascaux in France. This remarkable figure shows the ability of paleolithic artists to impart an uncanny sense of life to their creations. The paintings were always created far back in caves and were intended for secret magical rites connected with the hunt.

BIRDMAN: NASCA, PERU

This "Birdman" is one of a number of animal figures, including several birds, a spider, a snake, a whale, a lizard, and a llama, that have puzzled and amazed modern man. Some of these figures are as large as two soccer fields and can only be appreciated from the air.

TRIANGLE: NASCA

One of hundreds of huge triangles created by the Nasca, this one is bisected by a ritual pathway that actually extends for miles. Some of these mysterious geometric figures have an astronomical significance; others may have pointed to sacred objects on the terrain. This soil is too soft and the terrain too rugged to be the landing strips of ancient astronauts described in Chariots of the Gods.

PYRAMIDS AND BURIAL GROUNDS

Ascribe from the time of the ancient Mayans of Central America, the Old Kingdom Egyptians of the Step Pyramid, or the Sumerian city of Ur would have described his society as ordered and devout, in harmony with the gods and with nature. Modern people usually looks back on those same ancient people with a combination of awe and horror. We are impressed by the edifices they constructed—their pyramids, ziggurats, and temples. But we judge them by present-day concepts of right and wrong and with no small amount of condescension. Their great monuments seem possible only because of the suffering of thousands of captive laborers.

We see societies obsessed with death, with the most elaborate kinds of funeral rites. We recoil from the horror of human sacrifice connected with both ritual worship and with the burial of rulers. So much of the life of ancient man seems to have been a grandiose expression of the denial of death, or rather of death's not changing the privileged status of the ruling elite. It is difficult to grasp the extent to which ancient people believed that their rulers were gods, or that through elaborate, mystical rites, they became gods when they died.

The pyramids of Egypt and Mexico and the ziggurats of the Near East reflect these aspects of ancient life and death. Some cultures used them as places for the burial of the dead, and some did not, but each was located within a sacred precinct where worship, ritual, and burial took place.

All of these ancient memorials seem to be reaching to the heavens. The great ziggurats have been called pyramid-temples, but they might as well be called temple-mountains. To the peasants, artisans, and merchants who were not allowed to climb to the top of the structures, the ziggurats must have indeed looked like mountains, rising so far above the simple little buildings they lived in. Undoubtedly the rulers and priests meant them to tower over the masses, to demonstrate an immutable social hierarchy.

These were places for communing with the gods. They provided a way for a god to descend to earth, or a deceased ruler to step up to heaven.

All of this began with the Step Pyramid at Saqqara, near Cairo. Before this, Egypt's rulers were buried beneath the ground. But in the twenty-seventh century B.C., the architect of the Pharaoh Zoser constructed for his ruler a step pyramid for a tomb. The pyramid was so awesome that it was thought that the gods had assisted in its construction. This revolutionary type of structure was viewed as an actual stairway to the gods for the deceased pharaoh.

Ten miles south of Cairo on the opposite shore of the Nile stands the Great Pyramid, tomb of King Cheops, along with two smaller pyramids, those kings Chephren and Mycerinus. At first glimpse, seen under a dazzling Egyptian sun against the unrelieved desert landscape, they imprint themselves upon the imagination. Closer examination only serves to increase their wonder.

These pyramids, which date from the fourth Dynasty over 2,500 years before the birth of Christ, were built with the most rudimentary measuring devices. Yet the pharaoh's architects were so accurate in their calculations that the discrepancies in the length of their sides are only a matter of inches. Speculative theorists have suggested that the pyramids were sophisticated astronomical observatories in which internal proportions correlate to planetary movement.

The legendary tomb of the boy-king Tutankhamun yielded not only vast treasures but clear evidence of the essential Egyptian belief that there was no clear dividing line between life and death. In King Tut's tomb we find the jewels, artifacts, and utensils that would allow him to continue his highly privileged existence once he had, not "died and gone to heaven," but quite logically progressed, after the elaborate ritual of mummification and magical rites laid down in the Book of the Dead, to an afterlife where he would continue to

GLASTONBURY TOR: GLASTONBURY, SOMERSET, ENGLAND

An island in earlier times when the sea covered the low coastal area, Glastonbury is the site of one of England's earliest Christian communities. But of all the legends, myths, and mysteries surrounding Glastonbury Tor over the ages—the Tor, or tower, is all that remains of the ancient church of St. Michael—the most intriguing is that this is the fabled Avalon and that King Arthur and Guinevere are buried at an abbey below the hill.

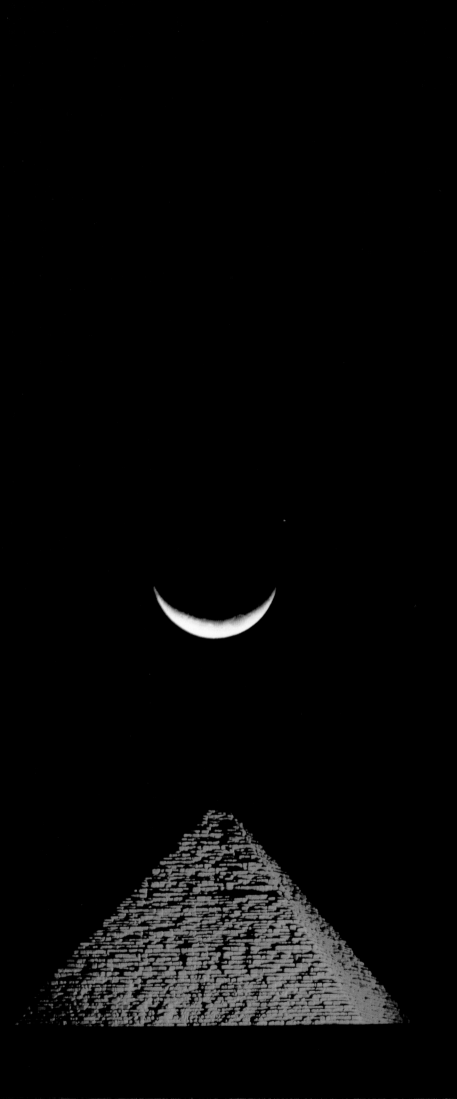

have need of jewels and to dwell in extravagant luxury.

The ziggurats of the Near East had no burial function but were meant to link man, particularly the ruler and priests, to the gods. One ziggurat even had a top step that was over three feet high, obviously meant for some god to step down into the temple from heaven.

Each of these ziggurats was surrounded by a sacred precinct of other temples and edifices, all concerned with worship and the coming death that would—through ritual and sacrifice—allow the ruler to pass naturally into an afterlife stocked with the riches, artifacts, and servants he was accustomed to.

For the ancient Sumerians and others who built the ziggurats, entire retinues of servants were sacrificed to serve their master in the afterlife. The death pits of the Sumerians at Ur—typical of those in other places—reveal not only riches but the bodies of seventy-four men and women, dressed in full court regalia, lying in neat rows, a little cup beside each body, nearby a copper cauldron. Apparently, these loyal retainers were so certain of their scheme of life and death that they willingly poisoned themselves to accompany their master beyond the tomb.

The horror such scenes arouse in us was in all likelihood not shared by these ancient cultures. For them, sacrificial rites were an integral part of their system of beliefs. In the same way, it must be remembered that not all the pyramids and ziggurats of Egypt and the Near East were built by wretched slaves and peasants, driven under the lash and threat of death, to aggrandize their pharaohs and kings. In Egypt, particularly, entire communities were built around constructing great monuments. The workers accepted as natural this labor ordered by a ruling class that had controlled the flooding Nile and made the desert fertile. They lived quite ordinary family lives for their times, in ordered communities in a tranquil land, and they were provided with grain and other necessities of life. And there is archaeological evidence that when the grain did not arrive on time, workers went on strike.

We know far less about the Mayan people of Mexico and Central America than we do about the Egyptians. But the Mayans have left us the ruins of impressive cities such as Chichen Itza and Palenque, including magnificent pyramids linked to astronomy, religious and funeral rites and complicated rituals involving human sacrifice.

At Palenque are remarkable stepped pyramids, each with a temple at its top. The most impressive, rivaling the finest Egyptian pyramids, is the Temple of the Inscriptions. At Chichen Itza, there are also impressive step pyramids, as well as huge recumbent statues holding trays where offerings from human sacrifices were left for the gods. There is also a well that has yielded the skeletons of some four hundred sacrificial victims.

It may be true, as a well-known work proposes, that all civilization is founded on the denial of death. But the widespread funerary rituals and careful elaboration of the details of the afterlife that characterize early civilizations suggest a willingness to confront elemental forces. Horrible as some aspects of these ancient societies might seem to us, we have reason to be grateful. Their obsession with death has left the world some of its greatest architectural works.

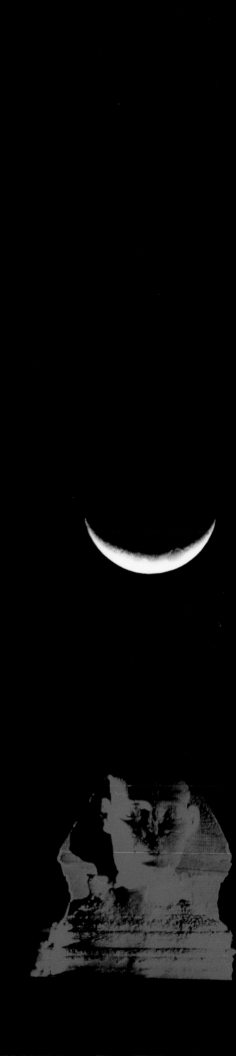

PYRAMID AND SPHINX:
GIZA, EGYPT

Many ancient people believed that only the gods could have constructed such awesome monuments and that plans for the Great Pyramid came down from heaven. Modern man has also voiced doubts that mere mortals with the skills and tools available thousands of years ago could have erected such edifices, arguing that extra-terrestrial visitors were the real builders. The ancient Greeks said that the pyramids were, indeed, products of the millennia-long Egyptian civilization, and that it took 100,000 men 30 years to erect the Great Pyramid.

THE GREAT PYRAMID: GIZA

The Great Pyramid is the only one of the Seven Wonders of the Ancient World still in existence. The most imposing structure in a sacred precinct of worship and burial, the Great Pyramid weighs some five million tons and is still the heaviest building in the world. It was built during the reign of the Pharaoh Cheops.

*When the tomb of King
Tutankhamun was discov-
ered in 1922, it was a rare
find—a tomb that had not
been stripped of its riches by
grave robbers. The mummy
was dressed in gold and
precious jewels and wore a
portrait mask of gold, inlaid
with turquoise, lapis lazuli
and obsidian. The body lay
in a gold-covered coffin that
was enclosed in a second,
solid gold coffin. And this
rested in a third gold-covered coffin covered with
semiprecious stones. The
mummy was surrounded
by an amazing array of
invaluable jewels, artifacts,
and furniture, and four
gold-faced chariots, all
intended for the king's lux-
urious life in the afterworld.*

STEP PYRAMID:
SAQQARA, EGYPT

Imhotep, the architect who designed the Step Pyramid at Saqqara, lived in the first half of the twenty-seventh century B.C. and was so revered by the Egyptians that he was considered a god. Many ancient people thought only a god could have conceived and built such a pyramid, which was the largest stone edifice ever constructed at that time. Surviving Egyptian texts suggest that the pyramid was built in steps to provide the king buried inside with an actual stairway to the afterlife.

OUTERMOST COFFIN, TOMB
OF TUTANKHAMUN: THEBES

Tutankhamun was a minor pharaoh. Given the richness of the appointments and artifacts that accompanied him into the afterlife, one can hardly guess at the vast wealth that must have filled the tombs of the great pharaonic rulers.

*This view of the Royal
Cemetery shows the relative
positions of the Tomb of
Tutankhamun and that of
Ramses VI. After Ramses'
tomb was discovered early
in the century, it was
thought that all the major
pharaonic tombs had been
excavated. It was due to the
persistence of Howard
Carter and the support
of Lord Carnarvon that
this most spectacular of
archaeological finds was
finally unearthed.*

STATUE OF THE KING, TOMB
OF TUTANKHAMUN: THEBES

Standing eroded on the stark desert now, in ancient times the Sphinx and the nearby pyramids stood in beautifully landscaped grounds that held plants and trees as well as many smaller pyramids, temples, and mausoleums.

SPHINX: GIZA

The Sphinx at Giza, carved out of the living rock, is 240 feet long and 66 feet high. The ancient Egyptians believed it to be the stone form assumed by Ra, the sun god, to protect his worshipers. Its face is not, as is generally assumed, that of a woman. It is perhaps a portrait of the Pharaoh Chephren in royal headgear.

PYRAMID OF SUN:
TEOTIHUACAN, MEXICO

Teotihuacan was the capital of an early pre-Colombian culture. At its height it covered eight square miles, was a flourishing center of religion, trade, and commerce, contained some of the New World's most awesome architecture, and then vanished from history. One of these edifices is the Pyramid of the Sun, which was once surmounted by a temple. Its base is larger than that of the Great Pyramid of Egypt.

PYRAMID OF MOON:
TEOTIHUACAN

*Like the Pyramid of the
Sun, this structure also
once had a temple at its top.
Unlike Egyptian pyramids,
these structures were meant
to be climbed, the temple
to be reached by the wor-
shipers after physical effort
and religious rituals.*

BABYLONIAN PILLAR:
UR, IRAQ

*This is one of the few
existing representations
of a priest standing before
a ziggurat.*

ZIGGURAT: UR

The ziggurats of the ancient Sumerians and Assyrians were built as "temple-mountains" and set amid sacred precincts of mausoleums and temples. They were places of worship meant, not only to provide a means for the priests to ascend closer to the heavens and therefore the gods, but also, because they towered over the small homes, to inspire awe and fear among the people. The great ziggurat at Khorsabad, built in the valley of the Tigris and Euphrates rivers, was composed of multicolored layers. The biblical Tower of Babel, built in the city of Babylon, famed for its Hanging Gardens, was a ziggurat.

CASTILLO:
CHICHEN ITZA, MEXICO

*The Castillo is a pyramid
that dominated the center of
the Mayan city of Chichen
Itza. Four exterior stairways
led to a temple at the top.
The Mayans were preoccu-
pied with the calendar—the
Castillo has 365 steps— and
every 52 years they
destroyed their temples and
built new ones. The Castillo,
however, is built over the
old temple. Human sacrifice
was a part of worship at
Chichen Itza, as shown by
large, reclining statues with
bowls for holding the hearts
and blood of victims.*

TEMPLES OF THE GODS

A temple is an edifice dedicated to the worship of a deity and thousands of temples have been built over the ages. But there are some temples whose sacred architecture uniquely encourages and houses that moment when a worshiper encounters the divine.

Chartres Cathedral is perhaps the most powerful and coherent embodiment of the Gothic spirit. It is famed for its enormous ceiling vault, which is so perfectly proportioned that it does not seem to bear any weight at all. Painstakingly executed sculpture tells the story in stone of man's fall and redemption. Throughout, Chartres is awash in the light radiating from its magnificent stained glass windows. The prelates who commissioned the cathedrals looked on them as representations of divine glory on earth. They closely followed the theology of Dionysius the Areopagite, which taught that God is Light and that as such He appears, more or less veiled, throughout His creation.

But Chartres contains even deeper mysteries. Some believe that a paleolithic well below the flagstone floor emanates telluric energy. In the third century, the Christians constructed a church here on a site long venerated by ancient man. This and four later churches at Chartres were destroyed before the twelfth-century masterpiece rose in 30 years of inspired and frenzied building. Without doubt the engineers and builders of Chartres possessed secrets that modern architects have forgotten. (The society of Freemasons traces its origins back to the guilds of the cathedral builders.) Their use of the principles of tectonics has created an architecture that elevates the

MAHADERA TEMPLE:
KHAJURAHO, INDIA

Of the eighty-five large
temples that once stood at
Khajuraho, in India, only
twenty survive today. All of
these splendid Hindu tem-
ples contain a profusion of
decoration and sculpture—
serpents and demons, gods
and nymphs and hand-
maidens—that create a
mass of undulating stone
beneath dome-like spires
resembling foothills and
mountain peaks.

TEMPLE CARVINGS:
KHAJURAHO

The most famous features of
the Khajuraho temples are
the mithuna of the ancient
Indian pantheon. These
sculptures of copulating couples may seem prurient to
the Western mind, but in
the Hindu belief they are
simply the decorative architectural aspects of a tantric
philosophy that views inter-
course as the manifestation
of creative and destructive
powers, a striving toward
spiritual union.

KONARAK TEMPLE:
ORISSA, INDIA

The dancing girl on the
steps of a temple at Konarak
recalls the temple courtesans
who embodied the marriage
of sensuality and spirituali-
ty that is so much a part of
Hinduism.

HYPOSTYLE HALL:
KARNAK, EGYPT

The Temple at Karnak, a religious center for some 2,000 years, was not simply considered a place of worship in our modern-day meaning, but the actual dwelling-place of the Egyptian sun-god, Amun. The Great Hypostyle Hall was the most important edifice in the temple precincts and is one of the largest chambers ever built. Its 134 columns, each 33 feet in circumference and 70 feet tall, were decorated with relief carvings.

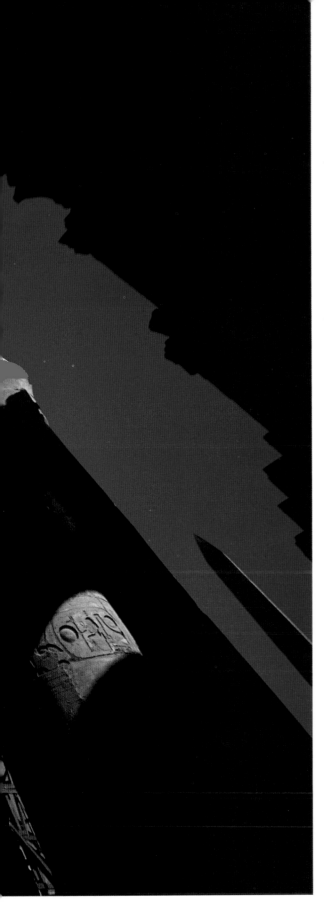

ENTRANCE TO TEMPLE: KARNAK

Karnak was composed of a series of courtyards, each entered by a monumental gateway called a pylon and decorated with flags. In addition to the complex of temples and ceremonial halls, there were sphinx-lined processional ways, carved columns, obelisks, stelae, and relief sculpture. The carvings depicted religious subjects, great battles, and the presentation of the spoils of war to Amun, and these great riches were stored at Karnak.

spirit of the worshiper and confirms the presence of the numinous.

Around the world, at Khajuraho in India, a devout believer can have his spirit and faith renewed in a temple that is equally uplifting, one that is permeated with the iconography of the Hindu religion. Despite obvious differences in architecture, decoration, and symbolism, these Hindu temples are considered the nearest equivalents to Chartres and other Gothic cathedrals. They share the same harmony of conception and the same feeling of spiritual aspiration. Like the great towers of the Christian churches, these Hindu temples are marked by magnificent spires. To a Hindu, a temple at Khajuraho is a sacred architectural mountain, identified with Mount Meru, the mythical peak where the gods dwelled.

HYPOSTYLE HALL: KARNAK

The great Hypostyle Hall was begun by Ramses I and finished generations later by Ramses II. Beyond the hall through the third pylon stands the largest extant obelisk in Egypt, which was built by Queen Hatshepsut around 1500 B.C.

But these temples of the Western and Eastern worlds are vastly different, for the Hindu temples at Khajuraho are filled with statues and high-relief sculptures of couples in explicit sexual acts. We in the West think of sex only in the physical sense of pleasure or procreation, but to the devout Hindu, worshiping among the profusion of stone erotica, there is a symbolism that goes far beyond the physical act and transports a true believer to a moment when he is best prepared spiritually to worship. To the Hindu, the erotic figures are concerned with the transformation of erotic energy into a higher plane. The artists who created the sculptures and the devout who worship among them believe that erotic energy can be changed into the birth of an inner person or spirit by religious discipline and meditation.

One of the most awesome and mysterious places of worship in the ancient world was Karnak, a complex of massive temples, processional avenues of ram-and-jackal-headed sphinxes, and huge ceremonial halls, dedicated to the Egyptian sun-god, Amun. Karnak was a religious center for some 2,000 years and would, within its elaborate, hushed precincts, have inspired

ANGKOR WAT: CAMBODIA

The temple of Angkor Wat in Cambodia may be the largest religious structure ever built. It was the symbolic dwelling of the god-king and became a magnificent tomb when he died. Isolated from the surrounding city by a moat, it was not built for daily worship by common people but for the quiet, contemplative devotion of priests for their gods and veneration of the god-king. Its many lotus-bud towers represented the mythical Mount Meru, center of the universe and home of the gods.

SMALL SHRINE: ANGKOR TEMPLE COMPLEX

King Jayavarman II began construction on the city of Angkor in the ninth century. It became the center of the Khmer empire, which spread throughout southeast Asia. It reached its height under the rule of Suryavarman II, who built the great temple of Angkor Wat. The temple complex included hundreds of other shrines dedicated to a religion that fused the Hindu pantheon with the cult of a god-king. The city was deserted in the fifteenth century and remains incredibly well-preserved, despite the centuries of encroachment by natural and human agents.

BET ABBA LIBANOS:
LALLIBELLA, ETHIOPIA

*This rock-hewn church
doesn't stand free. It was
cut into a natural cave.
According to legend, an
Ethiopian queen built this
church in only one night—
with the help of angels.*

CEILING PAINTING IN
DEBRA BERHAN SELASSIE:
GONDAR, ETHIOPIA

*Just outside the city of
Gondar (which was the
imperial capital of
Ethiopia's "Hidden
Empire" for 200 years)
is the church of Debra
Berhan Selassie, built
around 1700 A.D. The
church is renowned for its
paintings of biblical scenes.
Its ceiling (shown here) is
decorated with many rows
of angels' faces.*

in any worshiper a sense of being at that special time and place when he encountered his god.

But unlike such religious edifices as Khajuraho and Chartres, only the priests and the pharaoh — who was the high priest—could enter Karnak's temple precincts. Ordinary worshippers had their own popular gods, but they were forbidden the gods of the temples.

The priests made their devotions to Amun in such structures as the Great Hypostyle Hall. One of the largest chambers ever built, it could accommodate the Cathedral of Notre Dame in Paris and have plenty of space left. With its 134 stone columns, as wide as the spaces between them, faint light filtering in from windows above the columns, and elaborate relief carv-

ings on the columns looming out of the perpetual twilight, a priest would have performed his rituals in a massive space that was both sacred and dimly claustral. Standing alone before the statue of a god in the Great Hypostyle Hall, a priest would sense that he was in the presence of the divine.

Like Karnak, the temple of Angkor Wat in Kampuchea was not a place of worship in the conventional sense. It was not a public edifice in which worshippers congregated daily, such as Chartres. Angkor Wat was separated from the surrounding city by a moat. All these temples of the Khmer people, whose civilization reached its peak during the eleventh and twelfth centuries, were set apart from ordinary life: vast, quiet, magnificent temples for meditation and veneration of the god-king.

Angkor Wat may be the largest religious edifice ever built. Surrounded by its moat with floating islands of vibrantly colored flowers, guarded all around by 540 stone demons, it was the symbolic home of the god-king and became a magnificent tomb upon the ruler's death.

In its labyrinth of corridors, filled with carvings and sculpture, beneath many lotus-bud towers, the largest of which was 200 feet tall, Angkor Wat's priests lived isolated lives of contemplation. Believing in an amalgam of the Hindu and Buddhist faiths, these priests meditated and performed special rituals in the symbolic as well as the literal home of their god-king.

These temples, widely distant one from another in time and space, illustrate a common idea and practice. These examples of sacred architecture were conceived to exercise a transforming effect on the devotee and to make him receptive to the approach of his god.

PRINCIPAL TEMPLE:
MACHU PICCHU, PERU

This is the principal of the several temples discovered at Machu Picchu. Some of the Incan religious rites remain a mystery, but one of their main celebrations of the gods was held twice a year, at the solstices. The rites lasted for days and included animal sacrifices, prayers, coca leaf offerings, and a symbolic tethering of the sun to a ceremonial stone.

*The Andes Mountains form
a spectacular backdrop for
this Temple of the Three
Windows— so named
because of its three trape-
zoidal windows. The
temple's function in Inca
worship is not known, but it
may be related to a nearby
rectangular stone, believed
to have been a backsight for
observing the heavens.*

TEMPLE COMPLEX:
TEOTIHUACAN, MEXICO

*By the time of the Aztecs,
Teotihuacan had long
been abandoned. When
the Aztecs guided the
Spanish to these ruins, they
assured the conquistadors
that the city had been
built by giants. Some
archaeologists believe that
Teotihuacan is the earliest
pre-Columbian civilization
in Central America.*

DETAIL OF QUETZALCOATL TEMPLE: TEOTIHUACAN

This elaborate detail from the Temple of Quetzalcoatl shows the amazing boldness with which these mysterious people decorated their temples. The Feathered Serpent—Quetzalcoatl— alternates with the Fire Serpent, which bore the sun on its daily journey across the sky. The Aztecs named this awesome ruined city of temples, Teotihuacan, which means, "The place of those who have the road of the gods."

DETAIL OF QUETZALCOATL
TEMPLE: TEOTIHUACAN

*On the Avenue of the Dead
(named incorrectly by the
Aztecs, because the local
inhabitants cremated their
dead) is a six-tiered step
pyramid, the Temple of
Quetzalcoatl, the god who
represented the union of
land and air, heaven and
earth. Teotihuacan reached
its height during the period
between A.D.150 and 600.*

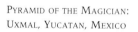

PYRAMID OF THE MAGICIAN:
UXMAL, YUCATAN, MEXICO

*Uxmal, in the Yucatan,
was the capital of the later
Mayan empire, and its
ruins, such as the Pyramid
of the Magician, show the
genius of Mayan architects
and stonemasons. Also
remaining from Uxmal's
days of splendor are a
round pyramid on an oval
base and a palace frieze that
was created from 20,000
dressed stones.*

HEAD OF IDOL:
SAN AGUSTIN, COLOMBIA

*Long lost in the verdant
green valley of the
Magdalena River, which
flows down from the
Andes Mountains to the
Caribbean, San Agustin
was thriving at least 2,000
years ago. It was aban-
doned around A.D. 1500.*

SINGLE STANDING IDOL:
SAN AGUSTIN

*The ruins of one of the
world's most enigmatic
cultures stand near the
town of San Agustin,
Colombia, 370 miles south-
west of Bogota. The idols
that remain are a complete
puzzle to archaeologists.*

POTALA PALACE:
LHASA, TIBET

*From this palace at Lhasa
in Tibet, the Dalai Lama
headed an elaborate hierarchy of monks (or lamas)
whose tenets of Buddhist
worship were combined
with an altered Sivaism and
local shamanistic rites. This
awesome monastery-fortress
in the high plateau of Tibet
has been called the remotest
place on earth. Isolated
from the outside world by
breathtaking mountain
surroundings, the lamas
developed powerful
spiritual practices.*

Overleaf
POTALA PALACE:
LHASA

*According to legend, the
Dalai Lama's palace is
connected to Shambhala, a
place of ancient wisdom
where people are immortal.
One of modern history's
greatest tragedies has been
the exile of the Dalai Lama
and the dismemberment of
Tibetan culture.*

SHRINES AND PLACES OF PILGRIMAGE

An eleventh-century caravan of weary Muslims struggles across the desert to Islam's holiest shrine, the Kaaba in Mecca, Saudia Arabia. A party of Christian cobblers and grain merchants, stone masons and wine vendors huddles in apprehension as it crosses the Pyrenees Mountains on a journey to Spain's shrine of Santiago (St. James) de Compostela. Javanese peasants are awed by what looms ahead, the base of Borobudur, a massive complex of temple-shrines dedicated to the Buddha, as they approach the end of their arduous trek. And nineteenth-century Jews from France are moved to tears as they finally complete their journey and pray at the Wailing Wall in Jerusalem.

For all of the major religions, certain shrines have exerted a powerful, mystical force to draw the faithful. These are usually ordinary people, and their pilgrimages to venerate a saint or sacred object may take months and are often filled with self-sacrifice, hardship, and danger.

Pilgrimages have been a vital part of religious life since ancient times. The devout of many faiths believe that a saint or a god should be venerated at a site he has had some physical association with. In Islam, the hajj, or pilgrimage to Mecca, is one of the five basic tenets of faith, and each Muslim is expected make that pilgrimage at least once in his lifetime. For most Christians, the pilgrimage is an individual act of conscience and choice.

Once the shrine is reached, the rites of the faithful vary greatly, though one additional common aspect at the end of the long journey is a ritualized miniature pilgrimage. As the pilgrim in Java finally ascends the steps of Borobudur, he is expected to continue walking around the ramps of the nine-tiered edifice as many as one hundred and eight times. At Mecca, the pilgrim, in a state of ritual humility and purity, circles and kisses the Black Rock embedded in the cube-shaped Kaaba seven times, while chanting devotions. The Christian pilgrim

STUPAS:
BOROBUDUR, INDONESIA

Borobudur, set against a dramatic backdrop of smoking volcanoes in Indonesia, is a temple complex containing the world's most impressive Buddhist stupas (monument-mounds containing holy relics or statues of the Buddha). Shown here are some of the 72 bell-shaped stupas on the higher tiers of Borobudur.

STATUE OF THE BUDDHA:
BOROBUDUR

Lower galleries of the nine-tiered structure contain more than 1,300 panels of relief sculptures portraying symbolic references to the Buddha's life. This magnificent and mystical work of Indonesian architecture in its volcanic setting has drawn pilgrims since it was built in the eighth century.

arriving at the great medieval cathedral of Santiago de Compostela enters through a prescribed side door and presses his hand into the sculptured genealogical tree of Christ—the tree has five indentations worn by centuries of fingers. The pilgrim ascends a staircase and embraces the statue of St. James from behind, then descends beneath the altar to look on the silver casket that holds the saint's bones.

One curious Christian practice over many centuries was the construction of mazes on church floors to represent the final journey to salvation. A penitent pilgrim, on his knees, would follow the maze, often called "The Road to Jerusalem," as his pilgrimage came to an end.

Jerusalem is a principal pilgrimage site for the world's three great monotheistic faiths. For some 1,000 years, Jews have journeyed to the Wailing Wall to bemoan their exile and the destruction of their temple and to write prayers on paper and slip them into the wall's cracks. The Church of the Holy Sepulcher has been revered and visited for more than 1,600 years by Christian pilgrims, who believe it is the place where Jesus was buried.

The Muslim faithful visit one of their religion's three most sacred sites, the Dome of the Rock, where it is believed that Abraham prepared to sacrifice his son, Isaac. Christians and Jews also venerate the huge sacred rock under the golden dome. Non-Muslims are allowed to visit there, though this has not always been true, and fundamentalists of all three faiths have tried to limit access to the faithful of their religion.

Scents such as musk were sprinkled on the golden dome's great rock so that the faithful who visited it could be distinguished by the scent. Pilgrims who completed the journey to Santiago de Compostela were allowed to wear the emblem of a scallop shell to show their devotion. No one knows the significance of this emblem, but as long ago as the twelfth century it was cut into the walls of some churches along the pilgrims' route. Some pilgrims over the ages have worn distinctive outfits that reveal which shrine they are visiting, such as the broad-brimmed hats of the medieval Christian pilgrims.

This silver statue is decorated
with inlaid translucent
enamels. The pilgrim holds a
reliquary of St. James. He
wears a wide-brimmed hat
adorned with a shell, the
emblem of pilgrimage.

Construction on Santiago de Compostela, the first great medieval cathedral in Spain, was started in 1074 to house the reputed remains of St. James. Pilgrims have traveled to Santiago for hundreds of years, to venerate the saint and marvel at such incomparable works of architecture as the Portico de la Gloria. The portico was carved in the twelfth century and shows Christ in Judgement with the saints. The cathedral is famed for its high altar, which is decorated with silver, alabaster, and jewels.

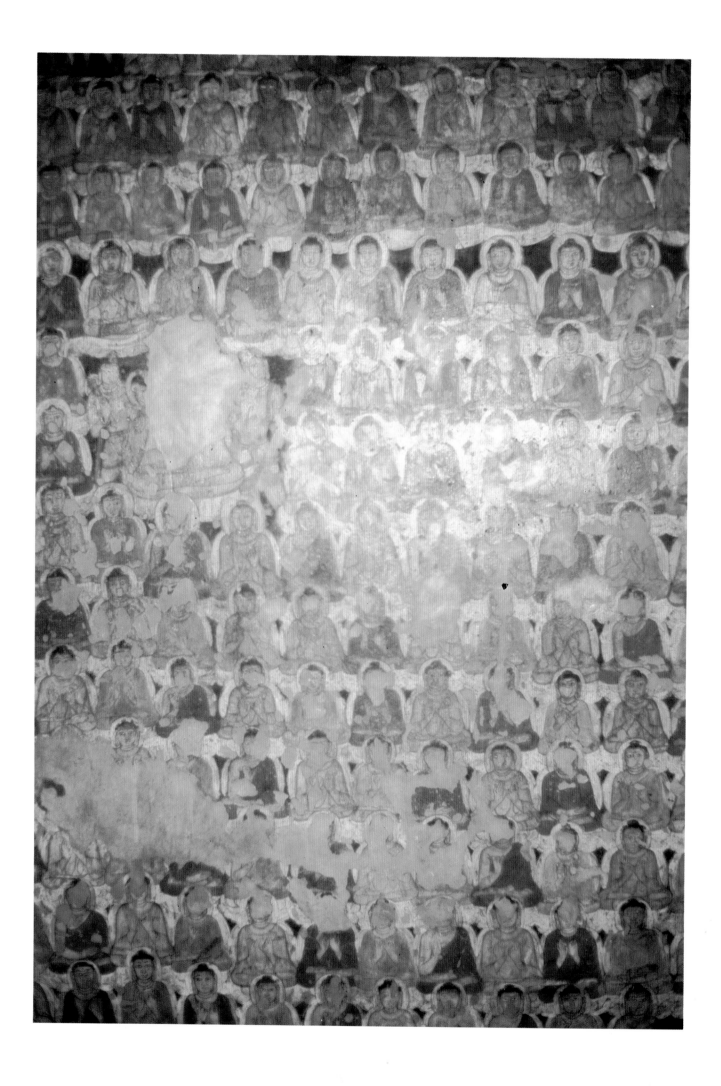

CAVE MURALS: AJANTA, INDIA

The Ajanta Caves in India, cut into a rugged gorge overlooking the Waghora River, had been deserted for centuries when they were discovered early in the nineteenth century. The architectural detail of the frontage dug out of the sheer side of the cliff is stunning; the insides of the caves, exquisite. The murals found there are among the finest in India. Four of the Ajanta Caves were sanctuaries where the community of monks met, and 25 were monasteries. The murals depict stories involving the life of the Buddha or subjects taken from the Jataka tales, which are accounts of his previous lives on earth.

KAABA: MECCA, SAUDI ARABIA

More than a million pilgrims journey to Mecca each year and gather in the courtyard of the Great Mosque to obey one of the five basic tenets of the Muslim faith. The center of their devotion is the cube-shaped Kaaba, draped in black brocade. In states of ritual purity, piety, and humility, they circle the Kaaba seven times and kiss the Black Stone embedded there.

DOME OF THE ROCK:
JERUSALEM, ISRAEL

Jerusalem is a major pilgrimage center for Muslims, Christians, and Jews. Muslims visit the Dome of the Rock (background), which they believe is the site where Abraham prepared to sacrifice his son, Isaac, and which is one of the three most sacred places in their faith. Christians and Jews also venerate the huge rock beneath the golden dome. In the foreground is the Russian Church.

WAILING WALL: JERUSALEM

For more than 1,000 years, Jews have traveled from around the world to Jerusalem's Wailing Wall, to lament their exile and the destruction of their temple and to slip written prayers into the wall's cracks. Although traditionally the stone blocks at the base of the wall are said to have come from Solomon's first temple, they are actually from the restored temple built by Herod.

GIANT BUDDHA: BAMYAN, AFGHANISTAN

Buddhism has always had a foothold in central Asia. Its teachings of self-abnegation, virtue, and wisdom began many centuries before the birth of Christ and spread to such remote places as this harsh landscape in Afghanistan, where a lonely caravan passes this gigantic statue of the Buddha, which is over 300 feet high.

SACRED MOUNTAINS, SACRED ISLANDS

The experience of the sacred is almost by definition something extraordinary, outside the parameters of everyday existence. That is why people have always looked upon mountains and islands as sacred places. Their separateness invites a corresponding separation from worldly concerns. They are the location of rites of passage, retreat, and mystical experience.

In a fundamental sense mountains and islands are archetypal images. Moses ascended Mount Sinai where he received the Ten Commandments, and according to tradition, the secrets of the Kaballah, directly from God. Siva is said to sit enthroned high in the Himalayas immersed in Yogic practices. The Ganges flows from the topknot in his hair. According to legend, King Arthur never died, but departed for the Isle of Avalon, whence he will return in the hour of England's need. These are but a few examples. Modern literature, from Thomas Mann's *Magic Mountain* to Robert Stone's *Outerbridge Reach*, sees the island or mountain as a crucible wherein the essential elements of human character are distilled and the dross burnt away.

Adam's Peak is a sacred mountain that rises more than 7,000 feet above the lonely, lush valleys of Sri Lanka and is distinguished by the mass of butterflies that swarm there each spring, as though on pilgrimage. Venerated by Muslims, Christians, Hindus, and Buddhists, the mountain's name comes from the Muslim belief that, when expelled from the Garden of Eden, Adam and Eve chose this land as the most beautiful place to live. On an oblong ledge at the peak's summit is a huge hollow that resembles a human foot. Muslims believe it is Adam's footprint; Buddhists, the footprint of the Buddha; and Hindus, that of Siva.

In a cave that bores into Ayers Rock in the Australian desert, boys are initiated in the rites of their Aboriginal people, rites that are so ancient that the Aborigines say they come from the Dreamtime, when the world was first formed. Ayers Rock and the Olgas, 20 miles away, are sunrise-colored sandstone monoliths that rise majestically from the desert. Each cave, indentation, lump, and crevice of Ayers Rock and the Olgas has religious significance to the Aborigines. These people, heirs to the longest continuing cultural tradition on the planet, have venerated these sacred places for countless millennia. Cave walls in Ayers Rock contain prehistoric drawings.

In ancient rites high in the Andes Mountains of Colombia, the heir to the throne of the Muisca people was covered all over with gold dust, placed on a raft with piles of gold and emeralds at his feet, and taken out onto Lake Guatavita where he deposited this votive treasure into the water. He was then proclaimed king.

Though this rite of coronation no longer existed when the Spanish conquered the Muisca, the conquistadors heard stories of gold beyond dreams of avarice and became determined to have it all. It was here, with the tales of the golden man and his treasure offered to the lake, that the legend of El Dorado was born. The Spanish did find gold in the mountains, but not the legendary amount they believed existed in the land of the golden man. They lost interest in the Muisca and their mountains, and El Dorado's lure soon led the Spanish to seek the fabled place in the Amazon jungle.

The island of Iona, off the coast of western Scotland, lay at the boundary of the Christian and pagan worlds when St. Colomba was drawn there from Ireland in 563 to found a monastery. It soon became the most important Christian community in Scotland. Norse raiders destroyed the monastery in the ninth Century, but it was rebuilt and was considered so holy that even the Norse worshiped there. A small island of austere landscape set in the lonely Hebrides, Iona has for centuries had a special religious significance and is the burial site of ancient kings of Norway, Ireland, and Scotland.

In 635, St. Aidan sailed from Iona to the island of Lindisfarne, off England's Northumberland coast, to convert that part

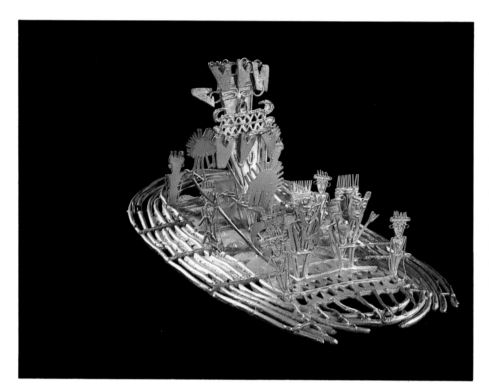

MUISCA RAFT

This exquisite, tiny golden sculpture was discovered by chance only a dozen years ago. The delicacy of execution of Muisca goldwork sets it apart from the other well-established stylistic traditions of neighboring tribes. The sculpture depicts a ritual in which the heir to the Muisca throne set sail on Lake Guatavita in a raft made of rushes to make offerings to the gods.

of England to Christianity. The monks of the place (long called the "Holy Island") created the magnificent Lindisfarne gospels, which are now in the British Museum. St. Aidan built monasteries and schools famed for their sanctity. Today Lindisfarne is inhabited by only a small community, but this austere island still seems to recall the spirit of its holy monastic dwellers.

One of the remotest and most mysterious places on earth is famed for gigantic stone statues that are as enigmatic to us as they were sacred to an ancient island people who no longer exist. Easter Island, 2,500 miles west of South America and 1,250 miles from the nearest island, has long been the center of a controversy over where its amazing stonecutters came from and in what way the long stone faces on their raised platforms were worshiped.

Though a strong case can be made that the original settlers came from South America, most archaeologists now believe they traveled from other Polynesian islands. Isolated in their remote home for centuries, the people of Easter Island developed idiosyncratic artistic and cultural forms. They cut statues from stone quarried from extinct volcanoes. Yellow-grey in color, the oblong faces were crowned with topknots of red stone. The statues range in height from ten to 32 feet and they all face inland.

It is generally believed that the statues were of clan or tribal chiefs and dedicated to some form of ancestor worship. In all, several hundred of the giants were quarried. The modern visitor feels the same disbelief and awe that they inspired in the first European visitors to this sacred island.

LAKE GUATAVITA,
COLOMBIA

*Believed to be the site where
El Dorado (the Gilded One)
washed gold dust off his
body while his followers
threw offerings of gold and
emeralds into the waters.
The cut in one end of the
lake was made by Spanish
conquistadors, who tried to
drain the lake and uncover
its treasures.*

ABBEY: IONA, SCOTLAND

St. Colomba traveled from Ireland to found a monastery on the Scottish island of Iona in 563. It was soon the most important Christian community in Scotland, and though St. Colomba's monastery was destroyed in the ninth century by Norse raiders—who later came to venerate Iona as a sacred island—it was rebuilt. Iona is the burial site for kings of Norway, Ireland, and Scotland.

LINDISFARNE CASTLE: LINDISFARNE, SCOTLAND

Lindisfarne, off the northeast coast of Great Britain, is known as the"Holy Island." St. Aidan arrived from Iona in 635 to convert this part of Britain to Christianity, and he built a monastery on the island. The island became famous for its sanctity and for the illuminated gospels created by its monks. This castle was built in the sixteenth century and later restored.

STATUE: EASTER ISLAND

Easter Island is one of the remotest places on earth, 1,250 miles from the nearest island and 2,500 miles west of South America. Though Thor Heyerdahl sailed his raft "Kon-Tiki" to the island from South America in an attempt to prove that the inhabitants traveled from there, most archaeologists now believe Easter Island's people came from other Polynesian islands in the Pacific.

These massive, enigmatic figures have haunted seafarers for many years. As early as A.D. 400, precisely carved stone blocks were erected along the Easter Island coast, and the statues, quarried from a volcano, were created on the blocks between 1100 and 1700. During the time the statues were being erected, the blocks became burial sites.

STATUES: EASTER ISLAND

Some 1,000 giant stone statues were erected on Easter Island, which is only 46 square miles of volanic land that can produce few trees and little vegetation, and at its peak could have supported no more than 3,000 to 4,000 people. This mysterious island culture somehow managed to quarry and create the giant faces using only the simplest stone tools.

One of the spectacular
Twelve Peaks of Wushan,
Goddess Peak is dramatical-
ly situated over a narrow
gorge cut through the
mountains by the Yangtze
River. It takes its name from
a rock at the top of its peak
that is in the shape of a
graceful nymph. Legend has
it that the young girl is the
incarnation of Yaoji, the
daughter of the Mother of
the Western Skies.

MT. ARARAT, TURKEY

This mountain in eastern Turkey, near the border with Iran, looms 16,900 feet over the isolated countryside. According to the Book of Genesis, it was here that Noah's ark came to rest on Mount Ararat after the Flood.

Defeated warriors once fled for their lives to the Pu'uhonua O Honaunau, or Place of Refuge, built in the twelfth Century and now marked by these two stone idols that reflect Hawaii's ancient past. This Place of Refuge also offered religious and political asylum.

KILAUEA VOLCANO, HAWAII

*According to legend,
Kilauea Volcano is the
home of Pele, the goddess
of fire. Ancient Hawaiians
believed that Pele vented
her wrath with furies of
sulfurous steam and
molten lava that erupted
from the crater at the peak
of the 4,088-foot volcano.
Charcoaled trees are
evidence of past volcanic
eruptions and ancient
lava flows show the
island's growth.*

AYERS ROCK, AUSTRALIA

The Aborigines believe that Ayers Rock was created by mythical creatures during what they call the Dreamtime, when the world was being formed. During Dreamtime, human-animal heroes labored through quests on which they discovered soaks and water-holes crucial to survival in the desert, and magical benevolent entities defeated such ferocious threats as the venomous-snake people and the devil dingo.

Ayers Rock is a sunrise-colored monolith that rises majestically from the Australian desert. Every crack, cave, indentation and crevice in this haunting sandstone mound has religious meaning to the Aborigines, who initiate their young men into tribal mysteries in a cave in Ayers Rock, as they have for millennia.

ROCK PAINTING:
AYERS ROCK

The caves of Ayers Rock provided a canvas for the Aborigines, who say some of their rock paintings go back to the mystical Dreamtime. Many of the paintings are linked to initiation and fertility rituals, while others of trees and fish show the Aborigines' respect for nature.

THE OLGAS, AUSTRALIA

The Olgas are an extraordinary outcropping of rocks located 20 miles from Ayers Rock. Sometimes called Mount Olga, these huge mounts of red sandstone are also sacred to the Aborigines and are a crucial part of their Dreamtime mythology.

TOMB AT ADAM'S PEAK:
SRI LANKA

Each spring, masses of butterflies swarm toward Adam's Peak, as though on pilgrimage. Thousands of human pilgrims of all faiths visit the mountain annually. The route to the peak is marked by chains said to have been put there by Alexander the Great.

ADAM'S PEAK

Muslims call this haunting mountain in Sri Lanka "Adam's Peak" because of the belief that when Adam and Eve were expelled from Eden they chose this land of mountains and lush valleys as the most beautiful place to live. Near the 7,360-foot summit is a huge platform that contains a large hollow resembling a human footprint, which measures five and a half feet by two and a half feet. Muslims regard it as Adam's footprint, while Buddhists and Hindus believe it to be the footprint of the Buddha and of Siva, respectively.

MONUMENT VALLEY:
ARIZONA/UTAH

The haunting vista of Monument Valley is one of the most spectacular in the United States. Long sacred to the Navajo Indian, it has become a part of the American imagination.

INDEX

PHOTO CREDITS

The publisher gratefully acknowledges the following sources for granting permission to use photographs in this work.

Australian Tourist Commission - pp. 118, 119, 120, 121

Marilyn Bridges - pp. 50, 5l, 52, 68-69, 85, 124-125

British Tourist Authority - p. 19

Jane Gladding Brown - p. 12 (bottom)

Rod Bull - pp. 10, 14, 15, 18

China National Tourist Office - p. 114

John Claridge - pp. 20-21

Colorado Tourism Board / Ron Ruhoff - p. 38 (middle)

© 1993, Comstock Inc. - pp. 2, 27, 32, 33, 45, 46-47, 70, 76, 77, 110, 111, 122, 123

Verlag Werner Dausien - p. 16 (top & bottom)

Egyptian Tourist Authority - pp. 58, 59, 62, 75 (top)

Victor Englebert - pp. 9, 34, 35, 36 (top) (bottom left & right), 37 (top & bottom), 64, 65, 70, 71, 78, 79, 80, 81, 82, 83, 84, 86, 87, 92, 94, 95, 108, 109

French Government Tourist Office - pp. 13, 48, 49, 106

Larry Dale Gordon / The Image Bank - p. 43

Greek National Tourist Organization - pp. 29, 30, 31 (top & bottom)

Hawaii Visitors Bureau / William Waterfall - p. 116, / Warren Bolster - p. 117

India Tourist Board - pp. 72 (top & bottom), 73, 100

Israel Ministry of Tourism - pp. 29, 102, 103

Landesamt fur archaologische Denkmalpflege Sachsen-Anhalt p. 17

Bud Lazarus - p. 40 (left)

Fred Maroon - pp. 22, 24-25, 28, 56, 63, 74, l04-l05, 115

Metropolitan Museum of Art - pp. 57, 60, 61

Mark Nohl / New Mexico Economic & Tourism Dept. - pp. 38 (top & bottom), 39 (top & bottom)

Ohio Historical Society - p. 44

Galen Rowell / Mountain Light - pp. 88-89, 90-91

Royal Jordanian Tourist Board - p. 26 (top & bottom)

Gary Sanson - p. 75 (bottom)

Tourist Office of Spain - pp. 98-99

Brian Sullivan - p. 12 (top)

Tahrike Tarile Qur'an - p. 101

Treasury of Santiago Basilica - p. 97

Pete Turner - pp. 7, 40-41, 54, 55, 112 (top & bottom), 113

Book designed by Adrian Taylor